# THE
# SECRETS OF
# FORTUNE
# TELLING

THE SECRETS OF FORTUNE TELLING

An Hachette UK Company
www.hachette.co.uk

Summersdale Publishers Ltd
Part of Octopus Publishing Group Limited
Carmelite House
50 Victoria Embankment
LONDON
EC4Y 0DZ
UK

www.summersdale.com

Printed and bound in China

ISBN: 978-1-78783-684-6

Substantial discounts on bulk quantities of Summersdale books are available to corporations, professional associations and other organizations. For details contact general enquiries: telephone: +44 (0) 1243 771107 or email: enquiries@summersdale.com.

DISCLAIMER
The author and the publisher cannot accept responsibility for any misuse or misunderstanding of any information contained herein, or any loss, damage or injury, be it health, financial or otherwise, suffered by any individual or group acting upon or relying on information contained herein. None of the views or suggestions in this book is intended to replace medical opinion from a doctor who is familiar with your particular circumstances. If you have concerns about your health, please seek professional advice.

# THE
# SECRETS OF
# FORTUNE
# TELLING

*A Beginner's Guide to*
*the Art of Divination*

ELSIE WILD

summersdale

# CONTENTS

Introduction ........................................................... 7

CHAPTER ONE: Reading the Body ........................... 8

CHAPTER TWO: Reading Nature ............................. 31

CHAPTER THREE: Fortune-Telling Tools .............. 52

CHAPTER FOUR: Tarot ........................................... 94

CHAPTER FIVE: Dark Divination ........................... 117

Conclusion ............................................................. 125

## ★ HOW TO USE THIS BOOK ★

As you read through this book and try out some of the fortune-telling methods, it's important to remember that free will (our ability to make our own choices) has a far greater impact on our lives than anything else – much more so than a deck of cards. Although it can be disheartening to receive a negative reading – which will happen from time to time – don't be discouraged. Think of divination as advice from the spiritual world or a nudge from your subconscious mind. It's simply telling you what *can* happen, but you and only you can decide what *will* happen based on your own actions. Take the advice from your divination, but don't forget to use your intuition to make the best decisions possible for you. Destiny is never written in stone, it is constantly written and rewritten by our own hands.

# INTRODUCTION

For centuries, humanity has searched for the answer to this elusive question: "What's going to happen next?" The world is unpredictable, so it's no surprise that people have chosen to shuffle tarot cards, gaze into crystal balls and search the stars for guidance and hope. We long to know if the choices that we make today will lead to happiness and success tomorrow.

Whether you have practised the art of divination before or are simply a little curious and want to know where to start, this book will be your guide to fortune telling – from palm-readings to Ouija boards – giving you step-by-step instructions for trying these methods for yourself. You won't become a seer overnight, but by practising these methods of divination, you'll become more intuitive, open and able to read the symbols that surround you in life.

Let's see what the future has in store for you...

## Chapter One:

# READING THE BODY

Our bodies can tell us a lot about our future: from the lines on our palms that look like road maps, to our birthmarks and the dreams that wake us in the middle of the night. None of this is random – it's the universe's way of giving us little clues to guide us toward our destiny.

It's a common misconception that fortune telling is a rare gift only a few possess – in fact, every single one of us has the ability to foresee our future, whether we're tapping into our intuition or reading the lines of our palms. Our magic comes from within, so in order to learn fortune telling we must start by learning about the power within ourselves. The markings on our bodies give us the first clues to who we are and where we are going.

# ★ PALMISTRY ★

Your past, present and future all rest in the delicate lines on your palms – your destiny marked on your flesh from the moment you were born. Palmistry, also known as chiromancy (from the Greek word *kheir*, meaning "hand"), is the practice of reading those lines on your hands and fingers to understand your past and to see what direction your life might take. In a sense, this is your own personal sneak peek into who you are and who you'll become. Your fate is literally in the palm of your hand.

Chiromancy is believed to have originated in ancient India, with roots in Hindu astrology. The practice then spread to other countries, including China, Persia, Egypt and Greece. The Greek philosopher Aristotle introduced palmistry to Alexander the Great, who then used the skill to judge the character of his army officers.

During the Middle Ages, palmistry was outlawed throughout Europe as it was thought to be a form of devil worship (although, ironically, palmistry was practised by witch hunters, who interpreted the marks on a person's hand to determine if they had made a pact with the devil). Palmistry was revived in the nineteenth century due to Victorian society's interest in the occult. Today, palmistry, along with tarot and astrology, is one of the most popular forms of divination.

## Reading between the lines

Each palm holds a different meaning. Your non-dominant hand (the one you don't write with) reveals your potential and what the future has in store for you, while your dominant hand (the one you do write with) shows what you've done with that potential so far. It is therefore important to read both hands.

In palmistry there are three major lines to read: the life, head and heart lines. These lines represent important events, life lessons, our character and our emotional life. As you know, you have many other lines on your hand, too, which we'll get to later.

This is the layout of the average palm:

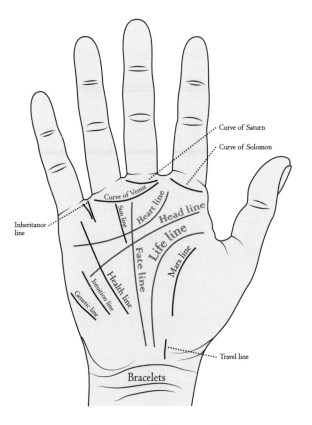

Curve of Saturn
Curve of Solomon
Curve of Venus
Sun line
Heart line
Head line
Life line
Inheritance line
Fate line
Health line
Mars line
Intuition line
Genetic line
Travel line
Bracelets

# ★ LIFE LINE ★

The life line starts at the edge of the palm between the thumb and forefinger, and curves around to the base of the thumb. Despite popular belief, it doesn't tell you how long you'll live (so don't worry if you have a short life line). In reality, the life line represents events in your life, as well as your physical well-being. Here's what you might learn from yours:

* **LINE RUNS CLOSE TO THE THUMB:** Chronic fatigue.
* **BROKEN LINE:** Struggles, losses and unexpected changes. A break in the life line on one hand may mean that you get sick and recover quickly. A broken life line on both hands may mean a chronic illness.
* **FORKED LINE:** Interruption and redirection in life, or sporadic bursts of energy.
* **LONG LINE:** Good health, stamina, vitality and a well-balanced life.
* **CURVED LINE:** High energy.
* **SHORT AND FAINT LINE:** Indecisiveness.
* **SHORT AND DEEP LINE:** Ability to overcome physical problems with ease.
* **NO LINE:** Prone to anxiety.
* **DEEP LINE:** Smooth life path.
* **FAINT LINE:** Low energy.

## ★ HEAD LINE ★

The head line (also known as the wisdom line) represents your intellectual pursuits, intuition and the lessons you will learn in life. In Chinese palmistry, this is considered to be the most important line. The head line starts just above the life line, between the thumb and the index finger, and runs across the palm from one side to the other. Here are a few things to notice when reading:

* **LIFE LINE AND HEAD LINE ARE SEPARATED:** You have a lust for life.

* **HEAD LINE STARTS ON THE LIFE LINE:** You are strong-willed.

* **CROSSES (SEE PAGE 18):** There is an emotional crisis in your life.

* **CHAINS (SEE PAGE 18):** You will have to make many difficult choices.

* **DIAGONAL LINE:** You are good at planning and self-expression.

* **LINE CROSSES ENTIRE PALM:** You are ambitious and successful.

* **STRAIGHT LINE:** You have an orderly and structured mind.

* **SHORT LINE:** You prefer physical adventures over intellectual ones.

* **CURVY AND FAINT LINE:** You have a short attention span.

* **DEEP AND LONG LINE:** You are a profound thinker.

* **STRAIGHT LINE WITH CHAINS:** You are a realistic thinker.

# ⭐ HEART LINE ⭐

The heart line, also known as the love line, deals with your emotional life and relationships. This includes your romances, friendships, sexuality and ability to commit. This line is located above the head line and is the highest horizontal line on the palm. When studying the heart line, here are a few things to notice:

- **LINE STARTS UNDER INDEX FINGER:** You will have a happy and satisfied love life.
- **LINE STARTS UNDER MIDDLE FINGER:** You will be restless in relationships.
- **LINE STARTS BETWEEN INDEX AND MIDDLE FINGER:** You fall in and out of love easily.
- **SHORT LINE:** You have little interest in relationships.
- **TOUCHES THE LIFE LINE:** Heartbreak hits you hard.
- **CROSSES THE FATE LINE:** You may experience relationship loss.
- **LONG LINE:** You express emotions well.
- **STRAIGHT LINE:** You are romantic.
- **PARALLEL WITH LIFE LINE:** You are practical in relationships.
- **CURVED LINE:** You will have many loves, but not many serious relationships.

# ★ MINOR LINES ★

As you can clearly see from your own hands, there are many other lines on your palm besides the life, head and heart line. These smaller lines also have a special meaning and can give you an inkling about your personality and future. Here are some other lines worth studying:

- FATE LINE: The fate line represents how much of a person's life will be affected by outside influences. It's also an indicator of how lucky a person is. The fate line is a vertical crease in the centre of the palm, near the life, heart and head lines. The longer and deeper the line, the luckier you are, and the more your life is likely to be affected by fate.

- HEALTH LINE: This line indicates how healthy you may be and your potential vulnerabilities. A straight line can represent good health throughout your life. If the line is deep with many crosses or chains, you may have to deal with some health concerns. If you can't find your health line, don't panic! This usually means you are naturally healthy and won't face any major issues.

- **MARRIAGE LINE:** This horizontal line is located on the outer side of your hand under your little finger and it represents your potential marriages. The longer the line, the longer your relationship will last. If the marriage line is curved upward, it may mean that you will remain single or marry later on in life. There can be more than one marriage line; the more lines there are, the more serious relationships you'll have.

- **FAMILY LINES:** These are vertical lines either under your little finger or between your little finger and ring finger, and they represent how many children you'll have, whether biological or not.

- **BRACELET LINES:** Bracelet lines are located on your wrist just beneath your palm. Most people have three bracelet lines. The first line represents health, the second represents wealth and the third represents possible fame. If you have a fourth line, it could mean that you will live to be a hundred years old. The deeper your bracelet lines, the healthier and wealthier you will become. If they are faint or have breaks, you may have some difficulties in those areas.

- **INTUITION LINE:** This vertical line is located on the left side of the palm. It starts below the little finger and finishes at the bottom of your palm. A well-defined intuition line represents great psychic abilities and a strong interest in the occult.

- **CURVE OF VENUS:** This is a curved line under the ring and middle finger that represents sensitivity and intensity in personality. People with this line tend to be more compassionate and open-hearted.

- **MARS LINE:** This line runs parallel to the life line, starting from inside the thumb. When a person's Mars line is deep they tend to be strong-willed with a big personality and lots of energy. This line also represents how attuned to the spiritual world they are.

- **THE "M":** An "M" is formed when the three major lines are connected by the fate line. If you can see the letter "M" on the lines of your palm, it is believed to be a blessing of good fortune. People with the "M" marking are also creative, motivated and a great judge of character.

# ★ IMPORTANT THINGS TO NOTICE ★

As you continue studying your palms, note down any particular lines, breaks or symbols that you see, as they could have a special meaning. Below are some of the marks you might see on your palms and what they could represent. You can interpret their meanings depending on which lines they occur.

**BRANCHES:** You will come to a crossroads.

**BREAKS:** You will experience weakness.

**CHAINS:** You will stray away from your goals.

**CROSSES:** You will face struggles.

**ISLANDS:** You will experience illness or injury.

**STARS:** You will have good fortune.

**SQUARES:** You will be protected from harm.

**TRIANGLES:** You possess psychic gifts.

**SPOTS:** You may face a crisis or bad accident.

# ★ NAEVIOLOGY ★

Naeviology is a divination practice that looks at moles, scars and other marks on the body (freckles, sunspots, etc.) to predict the future and give insight into our personalities. The word "naeviology" comes from the Latin term *naevus,* meaning "mole" or "birthmark". It has some roots in Chinese astrology, which claims our moles denote certain characteristics, and can appear as a response to the emotional and physical changes in our lives. Think about your own body's marks – the birthmark on your knee or the scar on your shoulder – as these could give you clues about your future.

## Mark location meanings

### Forehead

- CENTRE: Trouble communicating with important authority figures (parents, teachers, bosses, government officials, etc.).
- SIDE: A focused, driven and high-energy personality.

### Eyebrows

- UNDER EYEBROW: Sudden, abundant wealth from an unknown place.
- ABOVE EYEBROW: A steady flow of money throughout your life.

### Cheeks
- **RIGHT CHEEK:** Strong feelings and attachments.
- **LEFT CHEEK:** Possible financial problems.

### Ears
- **EARLOBE:** A good reputation.
- **INSIDE THE EAR:** Intelligence.

### Nose
- **END OF NOSE:** Relationship troubles.
- **SIDE OF NOSE:** Proficiency at handling money.

### Lips
- **UPPER LIP:** Enjoyment of the finer things in life (food, clothes, etc.).
- **BOTTOM LIP:** Successful children.

### Neck
- **BACK OF NECK:** Success in your career, but at the expense of others.
- **FRONT OF NECK:** Full of energy in body or mind.

### Arms
- **BELOW THE ELBOW:** A compassionate personality.
- **BETWEEN THE SHOULDER AND ELBOW:** Money coming easily.

### Chest

* Power in your career.

### Hands

* Skill in arts and vocations in which you use your hands.

### Legs

* THIGHS: A high sex drive and an extroverted personality.
* CALF: A tendency to burn out easily.
* KNEES: An ability to make money easily.

### Feet

* Leadership abilities and the desire to travel.

MEDICAL NOTE: As you examine your body for interesting marks and work out what they could mean, keep an eye out for moles that have recently appeared or look abnormal (i.e. if they have grown/changed, are discoloured or painful). If you see something that looks unusual, see a doctor to get it checked out. Don't rely on divination when it comes to your health.

## ★ CLAIRVOYANCE ★

Have you ever thought of a song and moments later heard it on the radio? Do you get goosebumps right before you hear bad news? If the answer is "yes", that's your clairvoyance coming through.

We all know the five senses: touch, sight, hearing, taste and smell. However, there is also a sixth sense: your extrasensory perception (ESP), also known as your intuition. It is this sense that allows us to practise clairvoyance: the ability to intuit things that are beyond the realm of our other five senses. Some people call this seeing with your third eye. Those who are clairvoyant may be able to glimpse future events, see into a person's past and present, detect spirits and communicate with them, and find things that are lost. With practice, you too can open your third eye and begin to see.

So, where is your third eye? Don't go looking around your body for it – your third eye is not visible, although many believe that it resides in the middle of the forehead, above the space between our eyebrows. The third eye allows us to unlock our psychic potential and gain insight into the spiritual world. Some people consider seeing with the third eye to be a state of enlightenment because it allows them to see *everything* – past, present and future – and unlocking that knowledge can help them to make better choices. The stronger our third eye, the better our clairvoyant skills become. But don't work it too hard or you could fall prey to delusions and headaches.

### Opening your third eye

So, how do we open our third eye and tap into our sixth sense? The good news is that we are all born with this sense, but some people have not yet fully activated it. Just like a muscle, it must be used in order for it to grow stronger, and the only way to make use of your natural clairvoyance is to make sure your body is prepared. To do this, close your eyes and allow yourself to relax and zone out. Don't try to think about anything deliberately. Instead, let thoughts and feelings come naturally to you, and then pay special attention to them – this is your intuition at work!

There are many ways to develop your clairvoyance – and there are tools to help (see Chapter Three) – but the most common and natural way to do it is by reading your dreams.

# ★ ONEIROMANCY ★

Have you ever woken up from the weirdest dream and wondered, "What could *that* possibly mean?" Maybe you spent your first waking moments trying to recall your dream because it was so bizarre you needed to remember it in detail, or maybe you told your friends about it. If you've done either of those things then you've already practised oneiromancy to some extent.

Oneiromancy is a form of divination that uses dreams to predict the future and it's a practice that's been used for thousands of years by everyone from psychologists to psychics. The word "oneiromancy" comes from two Greek terms – *oneiros,* meaning "dreams", and *manteia*, meaning "divination". Evidence from Mesopotamia dates the practice back to at least 3100 BC thanks to *The Assyrian Dream Book* – a group of ancient Sumerian texts relating to dream interpretation. Oneiromancy has since been practised by cultures all over the world, featuring in many religions – including Christianity, the Old Testament is filled with prophetic dreams – and in works of art and literature, such as the *Epic of Gilgamesh* and Homer's *Iliad*.

## The purpose of dreams

In 1899, psychoanalyst Sigmund Freud published the book *The Interpretation of Dreams,* which analyzed the hidden meaning of dreams and the subconscious. Though many researchers now believe that dreams serve to mediate memory consolidation and regulate our mood, still the fascination with our dreams continues.

Dreams occur during the REM (rapid eye movement) stage of sleep, and are made up of random images and sounds from our memories. Some believe that these are not just memories from our current life, but from our past and future lives as well. In divination, time is fluid and our dreams can give us a window into the future, allow us to understand warnings and provide answers to our burning questions.

## Preparing for oneiromancy

There aren't many ways to practise oneiromancy other than by simply going to bed, but you can prime your mind for dreams by meditating before you sleep and by opening your third eye to the possibility of receiving messages.

**STEP ONE:** Start with your regular bedtime routine. Turn off all electronic devices so it's easy for you to get into a relaxed headspace and you're not interrupted by a sudden text message.

**STEP TWO:** Place a notebook and pen on your bedside table within easy reach. This will be your dream journal. It's important to have the journal as close to you as possible so you can write down your dreams before you forget them.

**STEP THREE:** Get into bed and slowly close your eyes. Breathe deeply, in and out, in a slow, smooth rhythm, allowing your mind to wander. If you have a certain question you want answered, think about it as you breathe. If you don't have a question, just allow your mind to drift, without focusing on one thing, until you slip off to sleep. If you prefer to sleep with music on, make sure you choose something gentle and without lyrics.

**STEP FOUR:** As soon as you wake up from your dream, write down in your dream journal anything and everything you can remember: people, animals, colours, emotions, thoughts. Don't try too hard to remember exactly what happened in your dream, just write down everything that stood out and has stayed with you.

**STEP FIVE:** When you are fully awake, look at your dream journal and begin analyzing what your dream could have meant.

## For better sleep

Spray lavender oil on to your pillows to promote calm, relaxed and restful sleep. Lavender also banishes harmful spirits and helps to open your third eye. You could also sleep with a piece of amethyst under your pillow – this crystal promotes smooth communication between you and the spirit world, helps you to remember your dreams and also opens up your third eye.

> **FUN FACT:** Over a lifetime, a person may dream for five or six full years.

# ★ DREAM DICTIONARY ★

Dreams can mean many different things – interpreting them is more of an art than a science. Some dreams can be quite literal, while others are more symbolic. For instance, if you dream about a talking lion, the chances are that you won't actually meet a talking lion – but what does a lion symbolize in your life? Do you know someone with the sun sign Leo?

Here is a list of common dream symbols and what they could represent:

- **BABIES:** A desire for something new.
- **BEING CHASED (BY SOMEONE OR SOMETHING):** Feeling threatened or running from a problem.
- **BEING NAKED IN PUBLIC:** A fear of being vulnerable.
- **BEING TRAPPED:** Feelings of stress about a current life situation.
- **CAR CRASH:** Low self-confidence and a fear of losing something important.
- **CRYING:** The need to let go of emotions.
- **DEATH:** The end of something and the beginning of something new.
- **FALLING:** Losing control over your life.

- **FIRE:** Anger or unhappiness about a situation.
- **FLYING:** Independence and freedom.
- **FOOD:** That you have gained or that you need knowledge and energy.
- **GETTING LOST:** A lack of direction in life.
- **HORNETS:** Untrustworthy friends.
- **HOUSE:** Your body.
- **LOSING TEETH:** Loss of your power, youth or social status. It could also represent trouble with communication or that you have said something hurtful to someone.
- **PREGNANCY:** Fear of taking on new responsibilities.
- **TAKING AN EXAM:** Worries about the judgement of others.
- **SEX:** A desire or intimate connection with another person.
- **SNAKES:** Anxiety that someone is lying to you.

## But what if I didn't dream/can't remember my dreams?

Some people do not dream as vividly as others or may just forget their dreams as soon as they wake – and that's perfectly fine! Continue to practise. However, if you don't dream at all, this might be an indication that you're not sleeping well. If you are concerned, consult your doctor.

## Chapter Two:
# READING NATURE

For centuries, humans have been trying to divine their fortunes through the natural world – watching birds for messages from the other side, gazing into water for guidance and looking to the sky to see if our fate is truly written in the stars. Whether we are aware of it or not, the world around us will be trying to tell us something, sending us a message about what is waiting for us, if we would only slow down, listen and look.

In this chapter, you will find popular forms of nature divination as well as some methods that are not so common. So, read on and learn how to become one with nature!

## ★ ASTROLOGY ★

Whether you check it every day or just take a glance when you stumble across it, you've probably read your horoscope at least once in your life. But can that small paragraph based around the time you were born really be accurate?

Astrology, also known as astromancy, is the study of the astronomical positions of celestial bodies and their correlation with events on earth. Both terms come from the Greek word *astron*, meaning "star". By understanding the influence of the planets, astrologers believe that they can predict future events. From global crises to daily life challenges, it can all be found in the stars.

Astrology has been practised in many forms by many cultures over the centuries. The form referred to here is Western astrology, which can be traced back to around 2000 BC in the ancient city of Babylon in Mesopotamia. Babylonian astrologers used to track stars and planets to predict weather events and seasonal changes, as well as using them as a calendar. They believed that celestial events were how the gods communicated with the mortal realm.

In around 700 BC, Babylonian astrologers created a zodiac wheel, similar to the one we use today. When Alexander the Great conquered Babylon in 331 BC he was introduced to the concept of astrology and the zodiac, and brought back the ideas to the ancient Greeks. This is the reason the 12 zodiac signs we use today are named after characters from Greek mythology.

After the fall of the Roman Empire, astrology drifted in and out of popularity and has since been viewed in many different lights – from being a science, to being witchcraft, to being mere entertainment. Today, astrology is as popular as ever as more people look up to the night sky for answers.

# ★ THE BASICS ★

Astrology is different to most of the fortune-telling practices in this book because it relies less on intuition and more on observation and calculation. To begin the process of divining the future, astrologers study the movement and the position of planets, constellations, asteroids, the sun and the moon using an ephemeris – a device that gives the calculated position of a celestial object at regular intervals throughout a period of time.

To understand astrology, you are going to need to understand what the zodiac signs and the planets represent and how they move. Let's start with the zodiac signs. There are 12 in total.

 **ARIES:** Fire sign; first sign in the zodiac; ruled by Mars; represents passion, independence, innovation and enthusiasm.

 **TAURUS:** Earth sign; ruled by Venus; represents determination, loyalty, steadiness and a focus on material goods.

 **GEMINI:** Air sign; ruled by Mercury; represents communication, curiosity, sociability and intelligence.

**CANCER:** Water sign; ruled by the moon; represents sensitivity, a family-oriented personality, compassion and imagination.

**LEO:** Fire sign; ruled by the sun; represents boldness, self-expression, leadership and a flair for the dramatic.

**VIRGO:** Earth sign; ruled by Mercury; represents organization, hard work, observation and rationality.

**LIBRA:** Air sign; ruled by Venus; represents fairness, charm, artistic flair and a focus on relationships.

**SCORPIO:** Water sign; ruled by Pluto; represents mystery, transformation, ambition and magnetism.

**SAGITTARIUS:** Fire sign; ruled by Jupiter; represents spontaneity, philosophical ideas, humour and adventurousness.

**CAPRICORN:** Earth sign; ruled by Saturn; represents responsibility, discipline, maturity and career ambition.

**AQUARIUS:** Air sign; ruled by Uranus; represents humanitarian values, originality, eccentricities and a rebellious streak.

**PISCES:** Water sign; last sign in the cycle; ruled by Neptune; represents spirituality, kindness, creativity and subconsciousness.

## The planets

**THE SUN:** Although it's a star rather than a planet, the sun is significant in astrology. Our sun sign (also known as our star sign) represents our identity, ego and our true selves. It takes 30 days for the sun to move through a zodiac sign. It also has no retrogrades.

**THE MOON:** The moon represents our emotions, vulnerabilities and our comfort zones. It takes two and a half days for the moon to move through a single zodiac sign. Like the sun, it has no retrogrades.

**MERCURY:** The planet of communication, Mercury rules our thought processes, our interactions and the way we express ourselves. It takes about two weeks for Mercury to move through a single zodiac sign and it retrogrades three to four times a year. Mercury retrogrades can cause miscommunication, travel delays and technology meltdowns.

**VENUS:** Venus rules our relationships, the way we spend money and our attractions, pleasures and ideas of beauty. Depending on the sign it's travelling through, Venus can assert either a loving or a hedonistic influence over us. It takes four to five weeks for it to move through a sign and it retrogrades every 18 months. When Venus retrogrades, our relationships can take a turn for the worse.

 **MARS:** The planet of action, Mars rules our drive, willpower, energy and aggression. It encourages us to pursue what we want with determination. It takes Mars six to seven weeks to move through a sign and it retrogrades once every two years. When Mars retrogrades, our energy and motivation slow right down.

 **JUPITER:** The planet of luck, Jupiter represents fortune, growth, education, philosophy and the manifestation of opportunities. It takes Jupiter 12 to 13 months to move through a sign and it retrogrades approximately four months out of the year. When Jupiter retrogrades, it encourages us to look at everyday situations from a new angle to help solve our problems.

**SATURN:** Saturn represents restrictions, fears, hard work, and difficult lessons. It takes Saturn two and half years to move through a sign because it retrogrades every year for 140 days. In direct motion, Saturn is tough, but in retrograde its influence is rewarding.

 **URANUS:** Uranus represents unexpected changes, progress and a focus on the future. It takes seven years for Uranus to move through a sign and the planet retrogrades for six months out of every year. During retrograde, we're encouraged to end toxic patterns and reach for new ideas.

 **NEPTUNE:** The planet of imagination, Neptune represents spirituality, creativity and psychic powers. It takes 14 years for it to move through a single sign and it spends about 40 per cent of its orbit in retrograde. During this time, it pulls us out of our fantasies.

 **PLUTO:** The dwarf planet represents transformation, regeneration, obsession and hidden depths. Pluto takes 14 to 30 years to move through a sign and it retrogrades for 185 days a year. During this time, it encourages us to let go of harmful relationships and vices.

## ★ PUTTING IT ALL TOGETHER ★

### Planets and zodiac signs

When a planet is passing through a zodiac sign, the characteristics of that sign and the qualities of that particular planet influence one another. Therefore, reading the stars is a case of predicting what that combination could mean for your life.

For example, imagine that Mercury is passing through Leo. The planet Mercury represents expression and interaction, and the sign Leo represents boldness, leadership and a flair for the dramatic. When these two things are combined, it could mean that you will be particularly passionate and charismatic when speaking to others.

### Sun signs

The planetary movements are one half of your horoscope and your sun sign (or star sign) is the other half, as this tells you how you're likely to be influenced by the position of the celestial bodies. A passionate, confident Aries will be affected differently to an empathetic, romantic Pisces, for instance. (You will probably be familiar with your star sign, but if you're not, it's the zodiac sign that the sun was travelling through when you were born.)

## ★ THE BIRTH CHART ★

A common complaint of astrology is: "I don't relate to my sun sign!" If that's you, then you might want to consult your birth chart.

An astrology birth chart, also called an astrology natal chart, is a map showing the position of the planets on their journey around the sun the exact second you were born. It shows you the full picture: your strengths, weaknesses, personality and everything in between. So, if you have never identified with your sun sign, check out your birth chart and you may find that you have many different signs that explain your personality better. For example, your sun sign might be Libra, but perhaps your moon and rising signs* are Mercury and Mars respectively, which are moving through Virgo. If this is the case, you would probably relate more to Virgo's traits than Libra's.

*Your rising sign is the planet that was rising on the eastern horizon when you were born. If you don't already know yours, you can look it up online.

There are plenty of websites that can give you your full birth chart for free; all you need to know is your birth date, where you were born and the exact time. The time and location are very important because they help to give the most accurate chart.

While every planet in your chart is important, give special attention to your big three: the sun sign (how you understand yourself), the moon sign (how you understand your feelings) and the rising sign (how others understand you). These signs will have the strongest influence on you.

Once you understand your birth chart, you can make much better predictions. So, when you learn that Mercury will retrograde in Cancer in a few days, you will be able to start preparing, or you can plan out your romantic dates depending on which transits are most favourable to your signs, and so on.

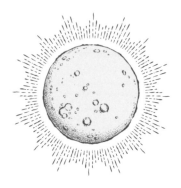

This is not the easiest method of divination to grasp and it may take many years to fully master. However, for those who choose to learn, the rewards are great, as you will have both an insight into what's up ahead and the good fortune that is only a transit away. Keep your eyes on the sky – you might learn a thing or two.

> **TIP:** When reading your daily horoscope in the paper or on a website, read the entry for your rising sign rather than your sun sign. Your rising sign steers your life just like your daily horoscope steers your day.

# ★ HYDROMANCY ★

Hydromancy is the art of using water, and its reflective surface, to see into the future or to receive messages. The term comes from the ancient Greek words *hydro*, meaning "water", and *manteia*, meaning "divination".

Hydromancy – also known as water scrying – has existed in various forms for thousands of years. One of the earliest recordings of the practice dates back to the early Roman Empire. This form of divination remained popular until the Renaissance when the practice was counted among the seven "forbidden arts" – along with geomancy, aeromancy, pyromancy, chiromancy, scapulimancy and necromancy* – and was therefore banned.

While hydromancy has never quite regained its popularity like chiromancy or astrology, this form of divination is excellent for beginners and those on a budget – because you just need to add water.

*Respectively, these arts involve predicting the future with: the earth; the wind and clouds; fire; the lines on a person's palms; a person's shoulder bones; and the practice of communicating with the dead.

So, why water? The element water has always been associated with intuition and psychic power, making it an excellent vessel to carry messages. In mythology, nature spirits dwelled in fresh water, so mortals would sit by rivers and lakes watching the ripples in hopes of a divine message.

## The ritual

To try water scrying at home, you will need the following:

- A black ceramic bowl (or a crystal or metal bowl)
- 1 tsp olive oil
- Water
- Candle
- Paper and pen

Take your bowl and fill it with water. Fresh rainwater is best because it comes directly from nature, but saltwater also works well because salt carries magical properties (such as purification and protection). Then place your bowl on a table or altar and light the candle. Dim the lights and settle yourself. Take a few slow, deep breaths in and out until you feel calm.

When you're ready, pour the olive oil into the bowl of water. Focus on the oily shapes forming on the surface of the water. Write down every shape you see and how it makes you feel. Finally, take your list and analyze these shapes to see what they could mean (check page 60 for symbol meanings).

## Water scrying tips

- Have a bowl that you use only for scrying. It can be kept with the rest of your witchcraft or divination supplies. (Don't try to eat from your scrying bowl when you've finished, you could confuse the energies and you might get a message in your alphabet soup!)

- If you wish, you could try using wax from the candle instead of the oil. (However, always exercise caution with an open flame and hot wax.)

- For a boost of magic, charge the water under a new moon (to do this, simply place your bowl of water in the glow of moonlight overnight). The start of the new lunar cycle is a good time to practise divination when we want to find out about new journeys and challenges.

- If you are scrying for love, place some rose quartz in your water to give it a romantic boost.

# ★ AUGURY ★

Many of us enjoy birdwatching as a hobby, but did you know that the birds could be sending you a message? In many spiritual and magical practices, birds have been held in high regard due to the belief that they bridge the gap between Earth and the heavens, and carry messages from the divine.

Augury is the practice of interpreting omens by observing birds and their behaviours. It may not be as well known as other divination practices, but it is in fact thousands of years old and has been used in many ancient societies: the Egyptians, Greeks, Romans, Celts and indigenous people of North America, to name a few, have all practised augury in some form. There is, however, debate surrounding the etymology of the term. It is thought "augury" could come from the Latin word for a clairvoyant, *augur*, or it could be a combination of the Latin words *avis* and *garrire*, meaning "bird" and "talk" respectively.

# ★ A LITTLE BIRD TOLD ME... ★

So, what are the birds trying to tell us and how are they getting their messages across? Often, birds will come when we need them – even if we don't know that we need them – bringing us messages on a variety of subjects, from love and relationships to pending danger. So, be aware of your surroundings at all times. Is there a bird that is not native to the area that keeps showing up in your back garden? Have you seen a murmuration of starlings on your way to work? Take notes in a bird journal, logging each of your sightings and noting the following things:

* Date, time and location.

* Type of bird (see the following page for some common symbolism).

* Number of birds (check the numerology section on page 87).

* Moon phase (for instance: a bird appearing during a waxing or waning moon could mean new beginnings or an ending).

* Emotions you felt.

* First impressions.

# ★ TYPES OF BIRDS AND ★ THEIR MEANINGS

Similar to crystals and herbs, birds carry their own symbolism that can help you understand the omens and messages they're sending you. Keep in mind that your environment also plays an important role. If you see a robin in an area with a high robin population, it may not mean much, but if you see a parrot in a place where they don't usually live, pay attention. (Or maybe someone just lost their pet parrot!)

- **BLACKBIRD:** A good omen.
- **BLUEBIRD:** A spiritual awakening.
- **CARDINAL:** A life-changing event.
- **CRANE:** Think with your head, not your heart.
- **CROW:** A bad omen (unless it cries three times, which makes it a good omen).
- **DOVE:** Upcoming marriage.
- **EAGLE:** Misfortune.

- **GULL:** Travelling.
- **HUMMINGBIRD:** Joy.
- **OWL:** Big changes (if it hoots three times).
- **ROBIN:** A guest will be coming later (if you see one in the morning).
- **SPARROW:** A happy home life.
- **WOODPECKER:** Success at work.
- **WREN:** Luck and your current situation will improve.

# ★ INTERPRETING A BIRD'S ACTION ★

Just as important as the bird itself is where it's going and what it's doing, as this can tell you a lot about future events. When writing in your bird journal, here are a few things to look out for:

- FLYING HORIZONTALLY: You will reach your goals, but it will not be an easy journey.

- FLYING LEFT TO RIGHT: You will achieve success easily.

- FLYING STRAIGHT TOWARD YOU: Your situation is quickly improving.

- FLYING HIGH AND FAST: You will experience quick success.

- FLYING QUICKLY AWAY FROM YOU: A delay in plans.

- FLYING ERRATICALLY: You may have unseen problems you need to deal with.

- CHANGING DIRECTION MID-FLIGHT: You will soon need to be flexible.

- FLYING AGAINST THE WIND: Someone in your life is not who they appear to be.

# ★ ALECTRYOMANCY ★

If you're living on a farm or in the countryside, then this next form of divination may be right up your alley. Alectryomancy is the form of fortune telling whereby a person observes one or several birds (preferably roosters) pecking grain that has been scattered on the ground.

The term comes from the Greek words *Alectryon*, meaning "rooster", and *manteia*, meaning "divination". Roosters have been used as a means of divination in many cultures around the world, from northern Central Africa to ancient Rome, as they were considered sacred animals that were connected to the gods.

## The ritual

For this ritual, you need at least one rooster and some grain. First, place your grain in the shape of individual letters on the ground. Create the whole alphabet if you can. Then, let your rooster(s) start pecking. Whichever letters they peck at are the letters you need to write down to discern meaning from.

If the idea of shaping grain into letters seems like hassle, another method is to place a rooster in the centre of a circle. Around the circle, place 26 pieces of grain – one to represent each letter of the alphabet. Write down each letter that the rooster eats and replace the grain so letters may be repeated. By the time the rooster stops pecking, you should have enough letters to make out a message (or at least have a well-fed bird).

## Chapter Three:

# FORTUNE-TELLING TOOLS

Our intuition, our bodies and the natural world can help us catch a glimpse of the future but, if you want to branch out, there is a whole realm of divination methods for you to explore that involve using other materials as tools to help you see. From crystals, to dice, to dowsing rods, this chapter will help you to seek out the future and understand what your findings tell you. For instance: what does it mean to see a weird shape in your teacup? And why is the number three always following you around?

As you go through this chapter, take note of the fortune-telling methods you are interested in trying out. Remember: some of these practices will work for you and some will not – and that's perfectly okay! This book encourages exploration and each individual must learn what works for them in their own personal practice.

So, read on to begin exploring a few magical objects.

# ★ CHARGING AND CLEANSING ★ YOUR TOOLS

When dealing with magic, it's important that you come to your practice with good energy, an open mind and an open third eye – and it's important that the tools you use have good energy, too. If you are working with a tool that has dull or negative energy, you are unlikely to get the results you want – and the tool may not want to work with you either. In order to imbue your tools with positive energy, you should charge and cleanse them before each use.

## Cleansing

Cleansing is the process of removing unwanted or negative energies from your object so that it's ready to take on new energies. It's particularly important to cleanse when you get a new tool (especially if it had a previous owner) and each time after an intense reading. Cleansing doesn't mean getting out the soap and disinfectant spray – you're cleaning it spiritually, not physically. Here are a few cleansing methods to try out:

**VISUALIZATION:** Visualization is a powerful method that's easy to do. Hold your object in your hand and look at it, imagining it covered in dirt and grime. Then, in your mind's eye, picture all that dirt and grime slowly melting away, leaving the object clean and sparkling.

**SALT:** Salt is a great cleansing tool to ward off negative energies. Cast a small salt circle around your object and leave it overnight; alternatively, you can sprinkle some salt over your object before you begin your reading.

**FULL MOON BATH:** The light from the full moon gives off a powerful, magical energy. Place the objects you wish to cleanse on a window ledge overnight to harness the effect of the full moon. When the sun comes up, your tools will be clean.

**SMOKE CLEANSE:** A smoke cleanse is the act of burning a bundle of herbs to ward off negative energy. Dried herbs such as rosemary, lavender and cedarwood work particularly well. To cleanse the energy, run the herb bundle past the object several times, making sure that the smoke covers the object.

**NOTE:** Always do extensive research before trying smoke cleanses and practise fire safety at all times.

## ★ CHARGING ★

Your electronics work best when they are fully charged – and so do your magical tools. Continuous use can drain your tools, making them slow and sluggish. When this happens, they may not give you the strongest predictions and there's a chance they won't give you any answers at all. If you really want to reap the full benefits of divination, it's important to have fully charged tools. However, unlike your phone or laptop, you can't just plug in your crystal ball somewhere. Here are few methods to get your tools to full power:

SUN BATH: Throughout the ages, people have revered the power of the sun, and its energy can certainly power up your teacup and tarot cards. Place your tools on a windowsill during the sunniest part of the day. When nightfall comes, your object will be charged and ready to go.

MEDITATION: Before using it, sit with your object in a quiet place at a time when you are content and full of positive energy. Hold your object in your hands and close your eyes. Slowly, breathe in with your nose and out through your mouth. After a few breaths, picture your energy flowing out of your body and on to your object. Do this for 5–10 minutes before opening your eyes again.

DANCING: The best way to become energized is to use energy! Put on your favourite song, grab the tool you want to use and start dancing. The energy you're using while dancing will transfer from your body to your object, not only charging it but also creating a connection between it and you.

# ★ TASSEOGRAPHY ★

Have you ever mulled over your problems with a cup of Earl Grey? What if it could answer back? The next time you go to wash your crockery, take a look – your destiny could lie at the bottom of your teacup.

Tasseography is the art of reading tea leaves found at the bottom of your cup to predict future events. If you aren't a tea drinker, don't disregard the practice just yet: you can use coffee grounds, wine sediments, hot chocolate and beer, too. By looking at the remains of your chosen brew, you can interpret the shapes you find and gain an insight into upcoming events. For example, if you see a clover shape at the bottom of your cup it can mean that good luck is coming your way. However, if you see a shark, it can mean danger is ahead.

The term "tasseography" comes from the Arabic word for cup, *tassa,* and the Greek suffix *grapho*, meaning "writing". So tasseography loosely translates as "writing in a cup".

The modern tea readings we are familiar with originated in Europe in the seventeenth century when the Chinese trade route brought tea to the continent. Once tea became more widely available, everyone could get a cup of divination – and the rest is history.

## The ritual

For a basic ritual all you need is:

- A teacup, mug or glass with a handle (preferably white or clear)
- Loose-leaf tea (or your drink of choice)
- A small plate or saucer
- Pen and paper

Prepare your cup of tea (or drink of choice) as normal, then drink until there's a small swallow of liquid left. Take the cup by the handle with your left hand and ask your question about the future. Swirl your cup three times counterclockwise. Then put the plate over the top of the cup and turn everything upside down so the cup is sitting upturned on the plate. Leave it this way for a minute so that the liquid can drain. Finally, turn the cup over and you should see your leaves at the bottom.

After you've completed the ritual, hold the cup out in front of you (with the handle pointing toward you). The cup is divided into three zones: the rim, the sides and the bottom. The rim represents the past/present, the sides represent upcoming events, and the bottom represents distant future events and an overall outcome. The handle represents you and what's happening in your home. The tea reading as a whole usually represents six months to a year in the future.

Read the cup clockwise, starting with the area of the cup closest to the handle. Write down anything you see in the leaves and where it sits on the cup. For example: an anchor (sides), an axe (bottom), a heart (rim), etc. Take a moment to let the information settle and meditate on your question before trying to decode the message. Then, when you're ready, take a look at the symbols guide on the following page.

- **ANCHOR**: Success in business.
- **BIRD**: Luck or a journey.
- **BOAT**: A visit from a friend.
- **BUTTERFLY**: A spiritual transformation.
- **CASTLE**: Unexpected fortune.
- **CAT**: Feminine energy.
- **CIRCLES**: Money and gifts.
- **CLOVER**: Good luck.
- **COMPASS**: Travel for work.
- **CROSS**: Troubles or hardships.
- **CROWN**: Success.
- **DOG**: Friendship.
- **ELEPHANT**: Luck and good health.
- **FISH**: Good news, fertility.
- **OWL**: Unlucky events.
- **PIG**: A faithful lover.
- **RABBIT**: Success.
- **RAT**: Loss.
- **SHARK**: Danger.
- **SNAKE**: A bad omen.

## ⭐ PUTTING IT ALL TOGETHER ⭐

Once you've completed your reading, written down everything you could see and have decoded the symbols, how do you know what it all means?

The answer is both simple and complex: it's whatever you think it means. Like most forms of divination, tasseography mostly relies on your own interpretation, because it's your personal message from the universe. For example, let's say you see an anchor, a boat, a crown, two fish and the letter L. This could mean a variety of things:

- You could have a successful visit from your friend whose first name starts with L.

- You could go on a business trip, meet someone whose name starts with L and get married.

- You could have two successful pregnancies.

Use your best judgement to see how the symbols fit into your life and what makes sense to you.

# ★ RUNE CASTING ★

Rune casting is a method of divination where runes – stones or small pieces of wood with ancient letters carved into them – are laid out in a pattern or randomly cast in order to solve problems and gain an insight into the future. Rune casting is a guidance tool that works with your intuition and subconscious, although some practitioners believe that deities, specifically Norse gods, can speak to mortals using the runes.

The term "runes" comes from the old Norse word run, which can be translated as "magic sign". The runes themselves are from the ancient alphabet Elder Futhark, which was used by Germanic communities before the adoption of the Latin alphabet in the late Middle Ages. However, according to Norse legend, the runic alphabet was created by Odin, the god of wisdom, poetry, divination and death.

There are 24 runes in a set, and they are typically made from the wood of a nut-bearing tree, or from stones and crystals. You can purchase pre-made runes, but many people prefer to make their own and carve or paint the symbols themselves, as it's often believed that this lends the runes additional magical properties. Similar to tarot (see Chapter Four), each symbol has its own special meaning that can be interpreted in many different ways. However, tarot and runes have two completely different ways of speaking to the fortune teller. While tarot deals in metaphors and specific details about the future, runic messages are often more cryptic and speak in riddles. Rune casting is like speaking to an ancient prophet, while tarot is like talking to your sassy but well-meaning grandmother.

# ★ READING THE RUNES ★ CHEAT SHEET

Each of the 24 runes has a wealth of meanings, but here are a few keywords to get you started.

ᚠ **FEHU:** New beginnings and wealth.

ᚢ **URUZ:** Physical or emotional strength.

ᚦ **THURISAZ:** Chaos, conflict and resistance.

ᚨ **ANSUZ:** Inspiration and communication.

ᚱ **RAIDHO:** Journeys and leadership.

ᚲ **KENAZ:** A guiding light.

ᚷ **GEBO:** Partnership.

ᚹ **WUNJO:** Joy.

ᚺ **HAGALAZ:** Divine intervention.

ᚾ **NAUTHIZ:** Restriction.

ᛁ **ISA:** Stillness.

⟨ JERA: Divine timing.

↑ EIHWAZ: Perseverance.

⟩ PERTHRO: Rebirth.

Ψ ALGIZ: Divine protection.

ϟ SOWILO: Completion.

↑ TIWAZ: Victory.

ß BERKANO: Growth.

M EHWAZ: Moving on.

M MANNAZ: Public image.

⎰ LAGUZ: Health.

⧓ INGUZ: Fertility.

⧫ OTHALA: Separation.

M DAGAZ: Insight.

# ★ CASTING THE RUNES ★

Like most forms of divination, the exact method of rune casting depends on the individual. For first-timers the basic ritual requires:

- 24 rune pieces (either wood, stone or crystal)
- A small closable pouch, big enough to hold all of your runes
- A small white cloth (such as a handkerchief)
- Pen and paper

Place your white cloth on the table, this is the boundary for casting (if any runes land outside of the white cloth, they are not counted). Take your small pouch of runes in your hands. Take a moment to clear your third eye. When you are ready, start shaking the pouch, mixing up the runes inside. As you shake, think of the question you want to ask. For runes, it's best to ask open-ended questions that don't need a "yes" or "no" answer. For instance, questions such as "What is my destiny?" or "What do I need to know about my current romantic relationship?" are good ones to ask.

For the actual act of casting there are a few different options. There is no right or wrong way to do it – simply do whatever feels natural to you at the time.

One method is to open the pouch and tip the runes out on to the table. The runes that land on the white cloth are the ones you read.

Another method is to take a handful of runes from your pouch and release them on to the table like dice. You would then read the runes that land on the cloth.

Using a tarot spread is another way to read runes. Simply open your bag and pull out your runes one at a time, placing them on the table in a certain pattern to answer a question (see Chapter Four for tarot spread ideas).

Once you have cast your runes, it's time to read them. Grab your pen and paper and write down the runes that come up and what they mean. Take your time interpreting the meaning, you can't rush divine messages.

# ★ LITHOMANCY ★

Crystals are not only beautiful, but they have the ability to influence our energies and the energy around us. As well as being worn as jewellery or used as a meditation aid, crystals can also be used for divination.

Lithomancy is the practice of using stones and crystals to predict the future. It comes from the ancient Greek words *lithos*, meaning "stone", and *manteia*, meaning "divination". The origins of lithomancy are uncertain. Some believe the practice has its roots in ancient Turkey, and others believe it originated in the pre-Roman era. However, the earliest records that mention lithomancy date back to the late 800s, when Saint Photios I of Constantinople described it being used in a ritual.

Similar to rune casting, the act of drawing stones from a pouch can provide guidance and insight into the future, but these crystals do not have symbols carved into them. Instead, practitioners use the symbolism already associated with the crystals to decode the message – or you can assign your own. It's possible to use lithomancy like a daily or monthly horoscope to see what is up ahead.

Lithomancy works best when you use small, round crystals that can be put into a pouch, shaken and rolled without fear of damaging them (so, leave your geodes and fragile crystals where they are right now).

If you don't have a crystal collection already, don't feel you have to run out and buy one. And if the thought of throwing your crystals around makes you feel uneasy, know that there are other ways you can do lithomancy. Objects such as stones found in nature, seashells, sticks and bones can also work as long as you assign them their own associations and meanings.

## Crystal associations

Crystals have special properties associated with them, and when practising lithomancy, these meanings can help you find answers, give you guidance and provide a glimpse into the future. For example, if you ask a question about your love life and pull out sodalite, you may have to focus on communication.

Here are some of the most common crystals and gemstones and their meanings.

- **AMETHYST**: Intuition, balance, trust.

- **AVENTURINE**: Prosperity, opportunity, good luck.

- **CITRINE**: Joy, creativity, abundance.

- **CLEAR QUARTZ**: Awareness, clarity, increase in energy.

- **LABRADORITE**: Joy, travel, innovation.

- **LAPIS LAZULI**: Wisdom, nobility, truth.

- **MOONSTONE**: Intuition, sensuality, travel.

- **RED JASPER**: Strength, honesty, stability.

- **RHODONITE**: Forgiveness, relationships, overcoming challenges.

- **ROSE QUARTZ**: Unconditional love, emotional healing, compassion.

## Assigning meaning

If you do not have a crystal collection you can use other materials such as stones, shells or charms, you just need to assign them their own meanings. Common lithomancy practice is to have 13 stones that represent each of the following categories: fortune, love, magic, news, home, life, Mercury, Venus, Mars, Jupiter, Saturn, the sun and the moon (check page 36 for the associated meaning of each of the planets).

It is up to you to choose what these categories represent for you. For example, casting the "love" stone could mean passion and romance, it could mean your current romantic relationship or it could mean self-love. Casting the "Mercury" stone could mean communication, or it could represent your sun sign. Just make sure whatever meaning you assign to each stone is what you stick to. You can also use this labelling system for crystals.

## Casting

The act of casting your stone can be done in a variety of ways. You can use the same methods as you do for rune casting (see page 66), or you can lay them out like a tarot spread (see page 113 for examples). You can also create a casting board.

A casting board is a board, cloth or piece of paper divided into sections and is used to make predictions depending on where the crystals fall. You can divide up your board however you like.

Ways to label this board could include:

- Yes, no, maybe, ask later
- Spring, summer, autumn, winter
- North, east, south, west
- Work/school, love, money, health

To cast, put your stones in a small pouch and shake them up with your question in mind. Next, open the pouch, scoop up your stones at random and toss them on to the board without looking. You can pull out a few or you can use all 13. After you have cast your stones, see where they have landed and make your own observations.

For example, if you have your board divided up into the categories of work, love, money and health, and most of your stones have fallen in the "love" section, expect a lot of activity in your love life in the coming weeks.

Remember that lithomancy is completely up to you, so have fun with it!

## ★ CRYSTAL BALL READING ★

Crystal balls are probably the most well-known fortune-telling tool. When you imagine a fortune teller, you probably envisage an elderly woman sitting in a tent at the fair, gazing into a clear crystal orb, claiming that she can see into the unknown. Many sceptics wonder if staring into a crystal ball can actually predict the future – but the answer is it can.

Crystal ball reading, also known as crystallomancy, is a form of scrying that uses the surface of a smooth orb in order to see the future. Practitioners believe that if you gaze into it for long enough, the crystal ball can awaken your psychic abilities.

Crystal balls have been used by clairvoyants since at least the first century AD, with the first known reference coming from Pliny the Elder who described crystal balls being used by "soothsayers" in ancient Rome. Crystal balls became increasingly popular in Rome over the next several hundred years until they were condemned by the Catholic Church.

Crystal ball readings then fell in and out of style over several hundred years until they became viewed as a cheap party trick. But make no mistake: if used properly, crystallomancy is a legitimate form of divination that can help you see into the future.

## Choose your crystal ball

Despite what you might think, crystal balls aren't always made of crystal. In fact, many of the crystal balls on the market today are made of glass. They don't have to be clear either – your crystal ball could be any colour or material.

When choosing a crystal ball, it should be at least the size of a grapefruit and it should rest on a small stand. Choose an amethyst, smoky quartz or lapis lazuli ball for an extra psychic boost. However, whatever material you opt for, the most important thing is that your crystal ball is reflective.

## The ritual

Place your crystal ball on its stand. Sit quietly for a few moments as you gaze into the ball, breathe slowly and deeply and allow your mind to wander. If you have a certain question such as "What will happen in my career?" or "What does my soulmate look like?", now is the time to visualize asking it.

Once you've relaxed, you might start seeing images appear in front of you. They can appear as wisps of smoke within the orb or as moving images – like film clips. Keep focusing on these images until they have run their course. Once they are gone, take some deep, calming breaths and write down everything you saw and the way each image made you feel.

## Decode the answers

As with most fortune-telling practices, the answer is rarely straightforward. If you see strange images in your crystal ball, don't take them at face value – it could be your intuition trying to tell you something. Take stock of how you felt when you saw them. Did you feel fear when a cat appeared in the orb? Did seeing a boat make you feel relieved? Try weaving together a story with the images you see.

Most of the time, the symbols that come up during scrying are personal and you'll have to use your intuition and mental associations in order to decode their meaning. However, here are a few common symbols and their interpretations to help you out (and check the tea-leaf symbols on page 60 as well):

* APPLE: Knowledge.
* BIRD: Good news.
* BOOK: Education.
* BUTTERFLY: Spiritual transformation.
* CIRCLE: Completion.
* CUP: Love and strong emotions.
* DAGGER: A warning.
* DOOR: New adventures.
* EYE: An awakening.
* KITE: Freedom.
* MOUNTAIN: Challenges.
* TREE: Relationships.

## ★ RHABDOMANCY ★

Rhabdomancy, also known as dowsing, is a form of divination that uses rods or wands to find water, gemstones, ley lines, missing objects and even grave sites. The term comes from the ancient Greek word *rhabdos*, meaning "rod".

Dowsing is typically done using one Y-shaped stick or two L-shaped sticks made out of hazel, rowan or willow (although copper or crystal sticks can be used as well). This form of divination works by tapping into your intuition, and the dowsing rods act as a receiver and transmitter for your energy.

When dowsing, a person holds the rod (or rods) in front of them in an open area and walks, keeping their arms straight. When the rods move up and down by themselves, it indicates that the person has walked directly where water, gemstones or the missing object can be found.

While not as popular as practices like tarot and astrology, dowsing is favoured by people who need to look for something specific, such as water, oil, minerals or ley lines. There is some evidence to suggest that the ancient Egyptians and the Chinese used a form of dowsing, but the practice as we know it today is thought to have originated in sixteenth-century Germany. Although a stigma developed around dowsing – it was frowned upon as a form of occultism – many Europeans continued to practise it and many people still do today.

## Dowsing rods vs witching sticks

Dowsing rods (or wands) and witching sticks generally refer to the same thing. However, when people talk about a witching stick they are usually referring to a Y-shaped stick, while a dowsing rod or wand tends to be the L-shaped rod that the user holds in each hand.

## The dowsing ritual

The dowsing ritual varies based on personal preference and purpose (i.e. whether the practitioner is looking for water or a lost item), but here are the basic steps to get you started.

**STEP ONE**: Cleanse your dowsing rod with your preferred method (see page 53).

**STEP TWO**: Find a spacious area with plenty of room to move. If you are looking for something specific, stand in the room or place where the missing item may be.

**STEP THREE**: Take hold of your dowsing rod. If you are using a Y-shaped rod, hold the stick at arm's length. For best results, lay it flat on your index fingers. However, you can also gently hold on to the handles if you prefer. If you are using two L-shaped rods, take one rod in each hand and hold your arms out in front of you, making sure they are a few inches apart. Keep your grip light and your arms as still as possible so as not to influence the rods' movement.

STEP FOUR: Ask your question, either out loud or in your head, then take a few deep, slow breaths, still keeping the question in mind.

STEP FIVE: Start walking very slowly, keeping your arms and the rod steady. Stop when they start to twitch.

STEP SIX: Start searching the area over which the rods moved. If you do find what you're looking for, congratulations! If you don't, pick up the dowsing rod(s) again and ask for more clarity.

Dowsing is a great tool to find things that are hidden from view, but even if you aren't looking for water, coal or your missing car keys, don't write off dowsing just yet. You can also use dowsing rods to ask "yes" or "no" questions, or for map dowsing (see page 86).

## ★ PENDULUM ★

If you're interested in dowsing, but would like something less conspicuous than a dowsing rod, a pendulum may be the perfect fit. A pendulum is a symmetrical, weighted object that is hung from a single chain or cord. The pendulum itself acts as a receiver and transmitter of energy, and moves in particular ways in response to questions. Similar to dowsing rods, pendulums can be used to answer "yes" or "no" questions, to find lost objects, to cleanse a room of negative energy and much more. If you so choose, you can wear your pendulum around your neck like a necklace so you'll always have it with you.

Typically, crystals are used as pendulums, but you can use any object that's not magnetic. If you prefer to have a crystal in your pendulum, it's best to use clear quartz (for clarity) or amethyst (for psychic ability). You also have the option of buying a pendulum or making your own.

## Programming your pendulum: yes, no, maybe so

Pendulum dowsing is a little different from other divination practices, as it has the ability to give you a "yes" or "no" answer. This is great if you are looking for quick answers, particularly as pendulum readings can be done almost anywhere.

However, before you let that pendulum swing, you need to do a little work. If you are new to this form of divination, or if you have a new pendulum, you need to programme your tool first. Programming means telling your pendulum what signals it should give you when answering your question.

To begin programming, sit down in a quiet room at a desk or table with your back straight and feet firmly on the ground. Clear your mind of any negative thoughts. Then, pick up your pendulum by the chain and with a straight arm hold it out in front of you.

There are two ways the pendulum can move, either by swinging (side to side or back and forth) or by circling (clockwise or counterclockwise). When programming your pendulum's "yes" and "no" response, you need to pick one kind of movement. For instance, don't try to programme circling clockwise for "yes" and swinging side to side for "no", otherwise your pendulum will get very confused.

Out loud to your pendulum, say the following: "When I ask a question and the answer is yes, move..." and then state the direction you would like. For instance, "back and forth" or "circle clockwise".

After that, wait for a moment. Then say: "Please give the answer for yes." If it gives you the answer for "yes", keep going. If not, go back and try again.

Next, do the same thing for "no", only this time give the opposite direction. For instance, if you said "back and forth" for "yes", you would ask the pendulum to swing "side to side" for "no".

Once you have programmed your pendulum, start by asking it questions that you already know the answer to, like "Do I have any pets?" or "Is today Tuesday?", especially if you are working with the pendulum for the first time. If it answers correctly, you can start working. If the pendulum is not responding or if it gives you a wrong answer, take a break and check your energies. Are you completely focused on the task at hand? Is your mind completely clear? Are you trying to push the pendulum to the answer that you want? Remember: the pendulum feeds off your energy, so if you aren't giving it the right kind it's not going to give you the help you need.

As you begin asking your pendulum questions, especially more complex "yes" or "no" questions, pay close attention to how it responds. For example, if you ask whether you'll be getting a promotion and your pendulum moves slightly to one side, you may be curious about what that means. Is it a maybe? Is it a no? Ask your pendulum for a stronger response or try to figure out what the pendulum is telling you. Maybe there's something about the promotion that you're overlooking.

## Types of "yes" or "no" questions to ask the pendulum

Not sure what to ask the pendulum first? Here are some suggestions to get you started:

- Am I on the right career path?
- Will I be successful as (insert career here)?
- Am I ready for a new relationship?
- Is my current relationship good for my emotional and spiritual growth?
- Is (insert divination practice) right for me?

## ★ MAP DOWSING ★

Map dowsing is an advanced form of dowsing used to locate something or someone on a map using a pendulum or witching stick. It can be done with any type of paper map, whether it's a small regional map or a world map. You can even dowse a map of the human body if you're asking health-related questions.

Map dowsing is a good option for when you want a general idea of where something or someone is. For example, if your cat is missing, pull out the map of your town. If you want to know where your next career move might take you, try using a map of your country or even the world for that answer.

To map dowse, hold your pendulum over the map and ask your question. Then, allow your pendulum to move across the map. If you feel it tug toward a certain location, you have your answer.

# ★ NUMEROLOGY ★

Do you have a lucky number? Have you ever made a wish when the clock hits 11.11? If the answer is "yes", chances are you've already experienced numerology on some level.

Numerology is the relationship between a number and its mystical presence on both an individual and worldly level. The term comes from the Latin *numerus*, meaning "number". We see numbers constantly in our lives, from important dates to the amount of money in our bank account. But numbers also hold spiritual value, so if a number keeps appearing in your life it's for a reason.

Numerology, and the idea that certain numbers hold significance, has appeared all over the world. In religion there's the holy trinity and 666 is the mark of the beast. Hanukkah lasts for eight nights. In tarot, the major and minor arcana are numbered, giving each card special meaning. In China, the number eight is lucky, but the number four is unlucky.

The best part about numerology is that you don't have to be a maths whizz to practise it. All you need is basic addition (or to have your calculator to hand) and you're ready to go!

## What do the numbers mean?

In numerology, single-digit numbers (1–9) have their own symbolic meanings associated with them and they give off a particular energy. When you see a certain number come up a lot in your life, it could mean that the universe is trying to send you a message. Here's a quick guide to what each number represents:

## Number meanings

1 Leadership, independence, pioneering spirit, innovation.

2 Compassion, balance, partnership, sensitivity.

3 Optimism, creativity, wit, self-expression.

4 Organization, honesty, hard work, tradition.

5 Adventure, change, curiosity, freedom.

6 Parenting, beauty, nurture, understanding.

7 Knowledge, introversion, spirituality, self-sufficiency.

8 Money, strength, authority, success.

9 Idealism, healing, completion, intuition.

Let's say you see the number 49 come up a lot in your life. Add the separate numbers until you have a single digit: 4+9 = 13; 1+3 = 4. This would mean that 4's energy has been following you.

## Life path numbers

Similar to the sun sign in astrology, each of us has a number that guides us through life called the life path number. The life path number is deeply important, because it's key to understanding our life's purpose, its gifts and the lessons we have to learn. So, how do you find this mystical number? With basic maths.

Add up all the numbers in your date of birth until you reach a single-digit number. For example, if you were born on 23 August 1994, you would add 2+3+8+1+9+9+4 together to get 36. Then you would add 3+6 to get 9. Your life path number is 9.

Work out your own life path number and see what destiny has in store for you.

### 1. *The leader*

LIFE'S MISSION: To take the lead and keep pushing forward into the unknown.

CHALLENGE: To overcome self-doubt and honour your unique voice.

### 2. *The peacemaker*

LIFE'S MISSION: To create harmony and build the bridge that brings people together.

CHALLENGE: To learn to put your needs before those of others.

### 3. *The creative*

LIFE'S MISSION: To express your true self to a captivated audience.

CHALLENGE: To develop the discipline to finish your creative projects.

### 4. *The teacher*

LIFE'S MISSION: To settle down and grow strong roots. To give your hard-earned wisdom to the next generation.

CHALLENGE: To not let your stubbornness prevent you from growing.

### 5. The adventurer

LIFE'S MISSION: To explore the world and expand your knowledge with each new discovery.

CHALLENGE: To not get carried away with self-indulgence.

### 6. The caretaker

LIFE'S MISSION: To take care of the people you love and keep them safe.

CHALLENGE: To learn that some things are out of your control.

### 7. The researcher

LIFE'S MISSION: To develop your skills and discover deep truths in life.

CHALLENGE: To let other people into your carefully curated bubble.

### 8. The CEO

LIFE'S MISSION: To be the boss of your own life.

CHALLENGE: To learn you can't replace love with material possessions.

### 9. The humanitarian

LIFE'S MISSION: To use your wisdom and gifts to make the world a better place.

CHALLENGE: To learn that endings are a part of life.

### Repeating numbers

When you see a number repeating not once but three times, this is usually the universe trying to tell you something important. So, pay attention. Here are what the numbers can mean:

111: It's time to manifest your desires.

222: Your mind, body and spirit are off balance.

333: You are on the path to your life's purpose.

444: What is meant to be will be, don't give up.

555: Big changes are coming up.

666: You need to reconnect with your spiritual side.

777: Good luck is heading your way.

888: You're about to get your good karmic reward.

999: Something is ending and it's time to let go.

# ★ SHUFFLEMANCY ★

If you are searching for a method of divination that's a little more up to date, give shufflemancy a shot. Shufflemancy is a modern tool of divination that uses the music on your smartphone to predict the future. To do this, you'll need your smartphone – or any music device with a shuffle function – and maybe a dice.

## The ritual

In a quiet space, focus on the question you wish to ask. Then roll your dice to get a number. If you do not have a dice, just pick a number at random or a number that means a lot to you.

Go into your entire music collection, or a certain playlist you enjoy – whatever feels right. Continue to focus on your question as you hit shuffle. Then, using the number you rolled, skip through the songs. For example, if you rolled five, skip five songs.

When you land on your song, listen and take notes. What are the lyrics saying? What is the mood of the song? What does the song mean in the context of your life?

## Chapter Four:

# TAROT

Tarot is one of the most well-known forms of fortune telling, and it's popular with long-time practitioners of divination and beginners alike. However, while we've all heard of tarot, it might help to explain exactly what it is.

Tarot is a form of cartomancy – the branch of divination that uses a deck of cards to look into the future. The term comes from the French word *carte*, meaning "card". A tarot deck has 78 cards, and each card has its own unique imagery and symbolism.

A tarot card reading involves laying out spreads of tarot cards. Spreads can vary in size, ranging from one-card spreads to 42-card spreads, and questions can vary from "What will my day be like?" to "What will my life look like in ten years?" Whatever your question, tarot is meant to provide not only insight into your future but also into the deeper truths about yourself, so keep this in mind when reading and asking questions.

Tarot cards have been used for hundreds of years, dating back to fifteenth-century Europe. However, these decks used to be used as playing cards, to play games such as Italian tarocchini, which is still played in parts of Europe today. The deck wasn't used for divination until the eighteenth century, when famed occultist Antoine Court de Gébelin popularized the idea that tarot cards were a form of ancient Egyptian fortune telling (although there's not much evidence to support the claim).

Thanks to a growing fascination with the occult in the nineteenth century, tarot started to become what we know it as today, with the major and minor arcana (the two main groups of cards in a tarot deck); individual scenes and a story on each card; and the four suits, pentacles, cups, swords and wands. Today's most popular tarot deck is the Rider-Waite deck, which was co-created by occultists Arthur Edward Waite and Pamela Colman Smith, and was first issued in 1910. The Rider-Waite deck is still the most recommended deck for beginners.

## Learning the deck

The tarot deck comprises 22 major arcana cards and 56 minor arcana cards. The minor arcana are divided up equally into four suits: pentacles, cups, swords and wands. Some decks may have different names for the suits (for instance, wands are sometimes known as batons, rods or staves), but there are always four different suits. Each tarot card has a special meaning assigned to it according to its imagery and symbolism. Further meaning can be derived from a card depending on where it's placed in a spread, whether it comes out of the deck upside down and the reader's own personal interpretation of that card. When getting to grips with tarot, it's important to remember that while you can base your reading on what each card represents, your own personal associations with the card and your gut response to its imagery is just as important.

NOTE: For a more in-depth guide to each tarot card's meaning, check the resources section at the back of this book (page 126).

## The major arcana cheat sheet

The 22 major arcana cards are the foundation of the tarot deck and each one symbolizes an overarching theme that can influence a person's life. When one of these cards appears in a reading, you should reflect on the life lessons it offers. If a reading is mostly made up of major arcana cards, this could imply that you are about to experience many big changes in your life.

0: THE FOOL: Unexpected opportunity.

I: THE MAGICIAN: The ability to manifest your desires.

II: THE HIGH PRIESTESS: Unexplored potential.

III: THE EMPRESS: Nurturing energy and marriage.

IV: THE EMPEROR: Ambition and authority.

V: THE HIEROPHANT: Learning practical lessons.

VI: THE LOVERS: Choices and growth in a relationship.

**VII: THE CHARIOT:** Overcoming challenges.

**VIII: STRENGTH:** Calmness through inner strength and courage.

**IX: THE HERMIT:** The benefits of time spent alone.

**X: THE WHEEL OF FORTUNE:** A change of circumstance (usually positive).

**XI: JUSTICE:** The need for balance and fairness.

**XII: THE HANGED MAN:** A situation that feels stagnated.

**XIII: DEATH:** Transformation.

**XIV: TEMPERANCE:** Moderation and compromise.

**XV: THE DEVIL:** Unhealthy relationships and overindulgence.

**XVI: THE TOWER:** Destruction.

**XVII: THE STAR:** Hope for better times ahead.

**XVIII: THE MOON:** Illusions and uncertainty.

**XIX: THE SUN:** Good fortune.

**XX: JUDGEMENT:** Reward for efforts.

**XXI: THE WORLD:** A triumphant outcome.

## Minor arcana cheat sheet

The minor arcana are grouped into four suits, each containing 14 cards. Unlike the major arcana, the minor arcana represent daily life and your state of mind rather than big-picture events. If your reading is made up of minor arcana, it's more concerned with everyday matters.

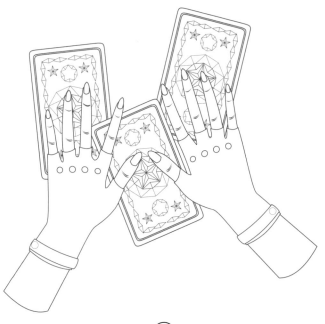

## Pentacles

Associated with the earth element, pentacles represent material issues such as money and possessions, as well as our feelings of safety.

- ACE: A new business opportunity.

- TWO: Balancing multiple responsibilities.

- THREE: Success through hard work.

- FOUR: Fear of loss.

- FIVE: Temporary hardship.

- SIX: Sharing or giving a gift.

- SEVEN: Investment and long-term plans.

- EIGHT: A new job; skill development.

- NINE: Financial success.

- TEN: Financial stability.

- PAGE: Good news; a studious child.

- KNIGHT: Hard work and productivity; a reliable young person.

- QUEEN: A capable, nurturing and practical woman.

- KING: Abundance; a successful man.

## Cups

Associated with the water element, cups represent our emotions, feelings and intuition. This is also known as the "relationship suit".

* ACE: A new relationship.
* TWO: Balance in a relationship.
* THREE: Happiness and achievement.
* FOUR: Boredom.
* FIVE: Feeling let down or betrayed.
* SIX: Old friends or lovers.
* SEVEN: Feeling overwhelmed by choices.
* EIGHT: Feeling emotionally unfulfilled.
* NINE: Wishing for fulfilment.
* TEN: Feeling committed and contented.
* PAGE: Happy news; a sensitive child.
* KNIGHT: Proposals; an idealistic young person.
* QUEEN: A sensitive and caring woman.
* KING: A creative and thoughtful man.

## Swords

Associated with the air element, swords represent the mental realm and how our thoughts manifest into realities.

- ACE: Triumph over adversity.
- TWO: A stalemate.
- THREE: Fighting with others.
- FOUR: Rest and recovery.
- FIVE: Hidden agendas.
- SIX: Harmony after a battle.
- SEVEN: A situation not going as planned.
- EIGHT: Feeling restricted by fear.
- NINE: Anxiety.
- TEN: The end of a cycle; failed plans.
- PAGE: Disappointing news; a difficult child.
- KNIGHT: Swift movement; a quick but serious young person.
- QUEEN: A no-nonsense woman.
- KING: A strict man of the law.

## Wands

Associated with the fire element, wands represent our creativity, actions, desires, strengths and primal needs in daily life.

- ◆ ACE: New ventures.
- ◆ TWO: Possible partnership.
- ◆ THREE: Progress within a project.
- ◆ FOUR: Stability.
- ◆ FIVE: Conflict and competition.
- ◆ SIX: Success.
- ◆ SEVEN: Overcoming obstacles.
- ◆ EIGHT: Progress after delay.
- ◆ NINE: The final push.
- ◆ TEN: Feeling overtaxed.
- ◆ PAGE: Good news regarding work; a cheerful child.
- ◆ KNIGHT: Changes at home; an energetic young person.
- ◆ QUEEN: Feeling busy.
- ◆ KING: Passion and leadership; an entrepreneurial man.

## Card reversals

A reverse card is when a card is pulled from the deck upside down and this gives it a slightly different meaning. It's not exactly the "reverse" of the original meaning – it may just take longer to achieve results than if you'd drawn the card in an upright position. For example, if you receive the Eight of Pentacles reversed, it may require more effort to advance in your job or to develop a skill, or perhaps you will meet more resistance than if you had received that card facing upright.

## Selecting your deck

Thanks to tarot's popularity, it's easy to find decks in a wide variety of designs and styles. While you really only need one deck, there are so many options that many people collect multiple versions and use them for asking different sorts of questions. For instance, you might use one deck for daily questions and another for questions about love and relationships.

However, there is so much choice out there that it's easy to become overwhelmed! If you're just beginning your tarot journey, a good choice is the classic Rider-Waite deck, as this is the one that most other decks are based on. You could also choose a deck that's heavily illustrated, as many people find it easier to learn tarot and gain insight by looking at the pictures. Once you become more familiar with the cards you can branch out with a minimalist or pop-culture-themed deck.

If you're hesitant about investing in a tarot deck, another option is to look into the various tarot apps that are available for your smartphone. While these apps aren't as intuitive as physical tarot cards, they are great for those who are learning tarot or want to do readings on the go. If you are artistic, why not design your own deck? Not only will it help you to learn the individual cards, but this will infuse your own energy within the deck.

## Bonding with your deck

Before you begin reading with a new deck, you must first bond with the cards. You're probably wondering, "How can you bond with an inanimate object? And why would you want to?" However, a tarot deck is no ordinary object – it is a tool that connects you with the spiritual realm and helps you tap into your intuition. Therefore, in order to yield the most accurate results, it's important to establish a strong personal connection with your deck. Trust is key to this relationship: you need to trust the cards to give you the right advice and, in turn, the deck needs to trust that you will listen to what it tells you. Without trust, this relationship cannot work. When people say they never get a "good" reading from tarot, it often means that they haven't taken the time to build a bond with their deck.

Decks also have personalities. Some are sassy, some are temperamental, some can be straightforward, while others are more cryptic. The more you bond with your deck, the better you'll understand its personality and the better your reading will be. For example, if your cards are sassy, expect some harsh but truthful readings. If your deck has a gentle nature, it may sugar-coat some of your readings.

Bonding with your deck takes time, but there are plenty of easy ways to do it. Here are a few ideas:

- Sleep with your deck under your pillow each night.

- Shuffle your deck absent-mindedly, allowing your energy to be transferred to it.

- Study the cards individually, not only memorizing the meaning of each card but also your own personal feelings toward them. Make up stories about each one to help you remember.

- Meditate while holding your deck.

Continue to do this as often as possible and you'll see an improvement in your readings.

## ★ THE READING ★

If this is your first time reading tarot cards, it's a good idea to start with a basic three-card spread known as "past, present and future". It's a basic reading that does what it says on the tin, but it's reliable and yields good results.

First, cleanse and charge your deck if you haven't already (see page 53 for details). Then sit down with your deck. You can practise tarot anywhere, but for your first reading it's useful to choose a quiet area so that you can focus. Keep a notebook and pen nearby so you can write down your reading and what it means.

Take your deck in your hands and clear your mind of all thoughts. If you have a specific question in mind, such as "What should I do about my career?", focus on it. If you don't have a question, simply remain calm and open. When it feels right, start shuffling your tarot deck. There's no right or wrong way to shuffle – do whatever feels natural. As you shuffle, visualize your third eye opening and the bond forming between you and the deck.

When it feels right, stop shuffling and deal three cards face up in front of you, as pictured above. The first card represents your past, the second card represents your present and the third card represents what your near future will look like – if things continue as they are.

> **TAROT TIP:** If you're shuffling and a card flies out of the deck, put it to one side and read it after you've finished doing your spread: it could be your deck trying to tell you something.

When you have all your cards laid out in front of you, grab your notebook and pen and jot down the cards you received. It's important to note that while the cards are dealt in the order of *past, present, future*, the cards should actually be read in the order *present, past, future*. This is because your present influences both your past and your future.

To begin reading the cards, first write whatever comes to mind and include your own associations with each card. Don't worry about making sense of it right now – just write based on instinct. After a few minutes of free writing, put down your pen, read over what you have written and start putting the pieces together. Think of tarot as a story written in code; the answer is there, you just have to figure it out.

Let's take this spread, for example:

PRESENT: Three of Swords: heartbreak and betrayal.

PAST: King of Wands: usually refers to a masculine figure who is viewed as a mature leader, or someone who is very passionate and driven.

FUTURE: The Star: hope for the future.

Remember that there are many ways to interpret your spread based on your own understanding of your cards and your current life situation. One interpretation of these cards could be that the reader is currently feeling heartbroken because they were betrayed by an ex-partner. However, there is hope for the future and their luck will turn soon. Another interpretation could be that the reader has just lost their job and is upset because their boss fired them – but there is hope for a new job in the future if they look for guidance.

## Crafting the right questions

What makes or breaks a tarot card reading isn't how the deck is shuffled or the type of cards you use, but the type of questions you ask. Tarot is open-ended, so your questions should be open-ended as well. Avoid vague questions and questions that can be answered with only "yes" or "no". For instance, "Will I be in a relationship?" can mean so many different things. (What type of relationship are you referring to? When will this relationship occur?) and "Will I be in a romantic relationship in six months?" is closed and doesn't leave much room for conversation or interpretation – and this could lead to your deck feeling jaded.

To craft the perfect tarot question you must word it as if you are asking a dear, trusted friend for advice. Try to remain neutral and open to an honest opinion. If you try to sway the cards into giving you a certain answer, they may just tell you what you want to hear and not what you *need* to hear. Tarot is a conversation, so be willing to listen.

Some good questions are:

- What can I do to develop a romantic relationship in six months?
- What steps can I take to get a promotion at work?
- What can I do to better my financial situation?
- What area of my life have I been overlooking?

## Spreads

As mentioned at the start of the chapter, there are many types of spreads that tarot readers use, ranging from one-card spreads to those that use every card in the deck. Spreads can be arranged to suit a variety of topics – friendships, career, self-help, monthly overviews or yearly overviews – and they can be as simple or as complex as you like. While larger, more complex spreads can provide a nuanced reading, one- and three-card spreads can answer a variety of important questions and help build your reading skills.

## One-card spread

This is the simplest spread in tarot because it's not really a spread – it's just a single card. However, even one card can provide insight and clarity, and another benefit is that it doesn't take long. Many people draw a tarot card each morning to glean a little wisdom about their day ahead, or one at night before bed to help them reflect on the day. Some good questions for a one-card reading are:

+ What do I need to know/focus on right now?

+ What do I need more/less of in my life?

+ What is my biggest block at the moment?

## Three-card spread

A three-card spread is a classic in tarot, and there are many uses for it beyond the past, present, future construction. Here are a few alternatives to try:

- Situation, obstacle, advice.
- What I think, what I feel, what I do.
- Where I stand, what I aspire to, how to get there.
- Yesterday, today, tomorrow.

As your reading ability grows, play with spreads and create your own.

## Other types of cartomancy

If tarot isn't your cup of tea or you would like to try your hand at something new, there are many other kinds of cartomancy to choose from.

### Oracle cards

Similar to tarot, oracle cards provide the reader with insight – but don't get confused, because these two decks are quite different. Unlike tarot cards, which have a strict structure, oracle cards have no rules. These cards can feature any kind of content and there is no set number of cards to a deck. While tarot gets into the finer details, oracle card readings tend to give you the "big picture" of your life and what you might be dealing with.

### Lenormand cards

If you don't enjoy tarot's open-ended answers, Lenormand may be the style of cartomancy for you. Lenormand cards consist of two types of oracle decks – the Grand Jeu, a full deck of playing cards with a large variety of symbols, and the Petit Jeu, a deck of 36 cards with very simple images (clover, bear, key, etc.). These images are very literal and perfect for "yes" or "no" questions.

### Angel cards

Angel cards allow the reader to seek insight and life guidance, and, as the name suggests, are illustrated with different angels. They are also considered to be gentler than tarot cards, putting greater importance on comforting messages than open-ended advice.

## Chapter Five:

# DARK DIVINATION

Fortune telling shows us the fine line between our mortal realm and the spirt realm. The more we try to use divination to connect with the other side, the finer that line becomes – and nowhere is this clearer than in the practice of communing with the dead.

Death has been a part of divination for hundreds of years. Early practitioners used animal sacrifices to divine the future or appeal to the gods for good fortune, and even today people attempt to reach the departed through mediums in order to receive messages or gain insight into the future.

The methods that we will be discussing in this chapter test the boundaries between the mortal and spirit realms, and invite you to consider the uncanny. However, it's a chapter that's more focused on history and possibility than actual practice. Dabbling in these kinds of divination is best left to the experts (because nobody wants to be responsible for a zombie apocalypse).

# ★ OUIJA BOARDS ★

Whether you consider it an instrument of the Devil or a board game made by a toy company, there's no doubt that the Ouija board has made a lasting impression in both divination and popular culture, providing years of inspiration for movies and fashion, and nightmares for teen sleepovers. But while we're all familiar with the concept of the board, how many of us know the truth?

A Ouija board – also known as a "spirit board" or "talking board" – is a flat board marked with the letters of the alphabet, the numbers zero to nine, and the words "Yes", "No", "Hello" and "Goodbye", along with various other symbols and graphics. Ouija boards are used during seances – gatherings where people attempt to make contact with the dead. To use a board, each person around the table lightly touches a planchette (a small heart-shaped piece of wood or plastic) placed in the centre and asks questions in the hope that nearby spirits will guide their hands to spell out a message.

Despite their sinister reputation, spirit boards were not originally viewed as evil or even creepy. In fact, the Ouija board that we know today was created in 1890 as a parlour game by American businessman Elijah Bond, and it was marketed as being a link "between the known and the unknown". At this time, the spiritualism movement was in full swing and many people wanted to talk to loved ones who been had killed during the American Civil War. During this period, communicating with the dead wasn't seen as strange – it was actually considered wholesome.

In 1901, Bond's employee William Fuld took over the production and renamed the board "Ouija", the name coming from the combination of the French and German words for "yes" (*oui* and *ja*). Ouija is a trademarked term, but it's still used generally to refer to many types of spiritual board.

The more popular the Ouija board became, the spookier the stories that started to emerge: spirits told people to make major life decisions, to allow evil spirits into their homes and even to kill. What sealed the Ouija board's fate was the 1973 horror movie *The Exorcist*, which showed a young girl becoming possessed by a demon after playing with a Ouija board by herself. The movie had a significant hand in changing the way people viewed Ouija boards, perpetuating the idea that they were a tool for Satan and creating a sense of fear around them.

Although the debate over the safety of Ouija boards is ongoing, they certainly can be safe to use, but only as long as you're careful – spirits don't take kindly to being disturbed.

**FUN FACT:** Many famous people throughout history have used a Ouija board to connect to the spirit realm, including poets Sylvia Plath and Ted Hughes, and veteran rock musician Alice Cooper, who took his stage name from a message his mother received via a Ouija board. Mary Todd Lincoln, wife of American President Abraham Lincoln, also held a seance in the White House.

## Basic Ouija board rules

If you are still interested in using a Ouija board, here are few rules you should always follow:

- Never use a board to disrespect the spirits.

- Never ask when you or anyone else will die.

- Don't believe everything the board says, especially if it's a spirit you don't know. Not all spirits have good intentions.

- Don't leave your planchette unattended on your board as that means you're leaving the door of the spirit realm open.

- Always end the session by moving the planchette to "Goodbye" and leave the room after packing up in order for the space to settle.

- If you start feeling some negative energy during a seance, quickly end the session and cleanse the board.

- Always make sure you are in a calm physical and mental headspace before using the board as it can have an effect on your energies.

# ★ NECROMANCY ★

Many of us understand necromancy as bringing the dead back to life – and this is certainly the definition in popular culture. However, it is a little more complex than that.

Necromancy is the practice of communicating with the dead either by summoning their spirit as a vision or by literally raising them from the grave. This is a moral grey area of divination and is generally not recommended.

The term comes from the Greek words *nekros*, meaning "dead", and *manteia*, meaning "divination", and the practice can be traced back to ancient Greece, Rome and Persia. An early appearance of the idea of necromancy is in Homer's *Odyssey* when Odysseus travelled to the underworld in order to receive a prophecy about his upcoming voyage. Since then, necromancy has appeared in art and literature in various forms, from epic poems to zombie films.

The rituals of communicating with the dead have varied with each practitioner and culture. Some involved wands, spell work and casting magic circles, while other rituals required clothing, items or possessions of the dead person that the practitioner wished to speak to or reanimate. Some rituals involved leaving food and drink out for the spirits to consume. There are also plenty of other rituals, far too gruesome to detail here. It wasn't until the medieval period that necromancy became associated with dark magic and was condemned by the Church (even though it was still highly popular).

## What do the dead really know?

So, why do we want to talk to the dead? One reason is purely emotional: we want to connect with our loved ones who are no longer with us physically and for many people their dearest wish is to bring them back to life. Another reason is the belief that the dead have knowledge they could impart to us. Time is not linear for the spirit world and those on the other side can see into the past, present and future.

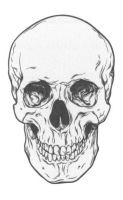

We can see this idea played out in Ovid's *Metamorphoses*, in which the underworld is shown to be a marketplace of knowledge and insight.

While using necromancy to raise the dead is rarely practised any more, it's possible that witches and spiritualists may still go to graveyards to cast spells and summon other worldly beings for advice. However, if horror movies have taught us anything it's that it's best to leave the dead in peace.

# CONCLUSION

The world of fortune telling is full of possibility. Having read through the practices in this book, it's now time to go forth and try these methods for yourself. You may already know what you want to do – perhaps you felt an affinity with palmistry or a pull toward tarot – or you may want to explore different methods and see what feels best for you. Maybe you will find a new calling or learn something new about yourself along the way. Or perhaps you will simply discover something fun to do with your friends.

Whatever you plan to do now you have finished this book, hopefully you will have learned to trust your intuition a little bit more than you did before, and your heart, mind and, most importantly, your third eye will be a little more open. Remember: your destiny is always in your hands. Divination is meant to give you guidance in times of need and a little push in the right direction.

Good luck and may your future always be bright.

# ⭐ RESOURCES ⭐

If you are interested in learning more about fortune telling, here are some great resources:

### Palm reading

Eason, Cassandra *A Little Bit of Palmistry* (2018, Sterling Ethos)

Struthers, Jane *The Palmistry Bible: The Definitive Guide to Hand Reading* (2005, Sterling Ethos)

### Oneiromancy

Cornwall, Lizzie *The Little Book of Dreams* (2018, Summersdale)

Ryan, Briceida *The Ultimate Dictionary of Dream Language* (2013, Hampton Roads)

### Astrology

Williamson, Marion *The Little Book of Astrology* (2017, Summersdale)

Williamson, Marion *The Little Book of the Zodiac* (2018, Summersdale)

Woolfolk, Joanna Martine *The Only Astrology Book You'll Ever Need* (2012, Taylor Trade)

Astro.com (for a birth chart)